Eleanor Gamble

3.50

3/1/W

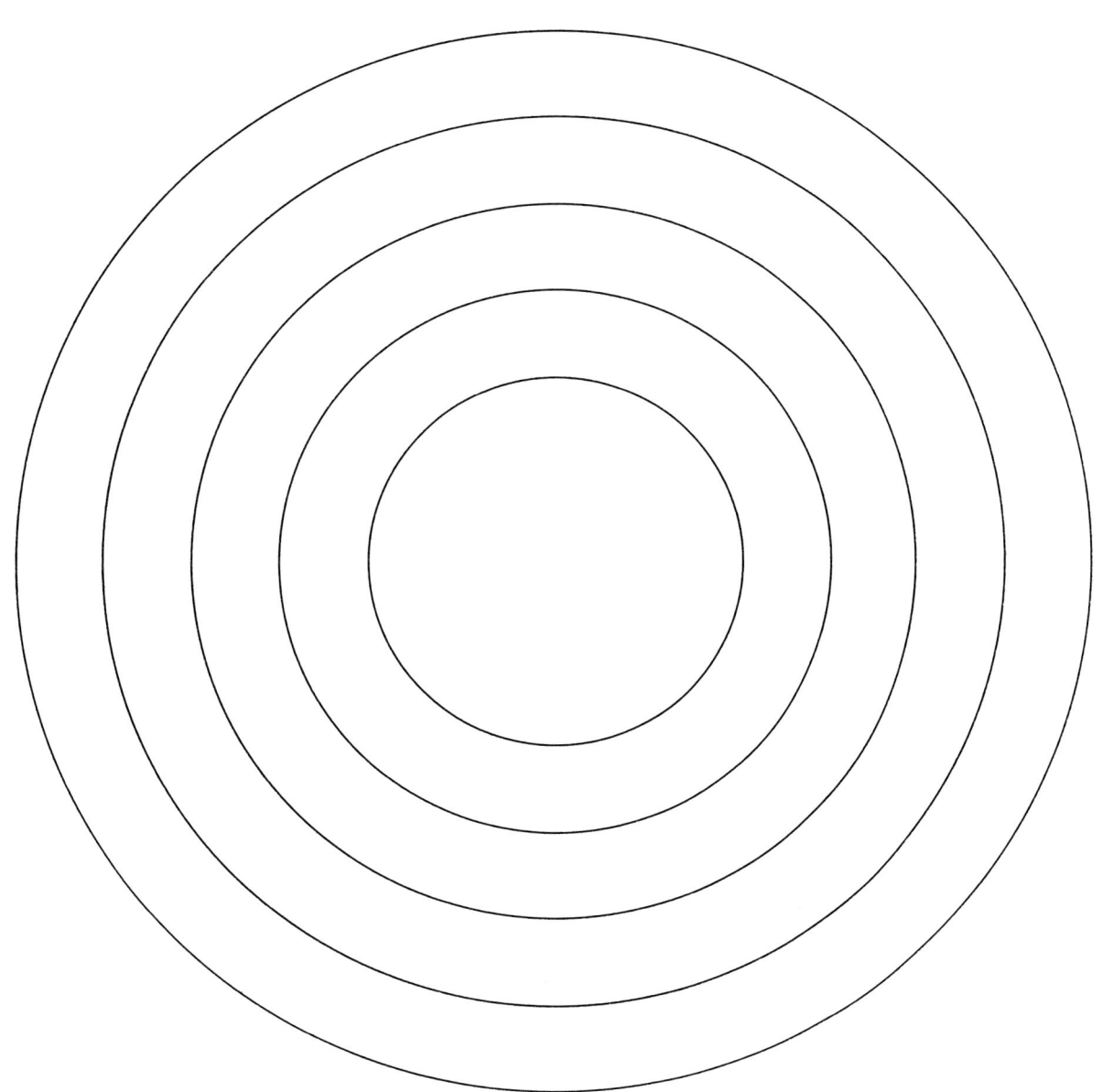

**Thank God for Circles**

THANK GOD FOR CIRCLES
Copyright 1971 Augsburg Publishing House
Library of Congress Catalog Card No. 75-159012
International Standard Book No. 0-8066-1135-9
All rights reserved.
Manufactured in the United States of America

# Thank God for Circles

STORY BY JOANNE MARXHAUSEN
ART BY DAN JOHNSON

AUGSBURG PUBLISHING HOUSE • MINNEAPOLIS, MINNESOTA

A line starts here . . .

and it stops.

But a circle just is.  It doesn't begin and it doesn't end.　　　A circle is like God—no beginning, no end.

Like a circle God just is...

forever.

Round things remind us of circles and forever and God and things

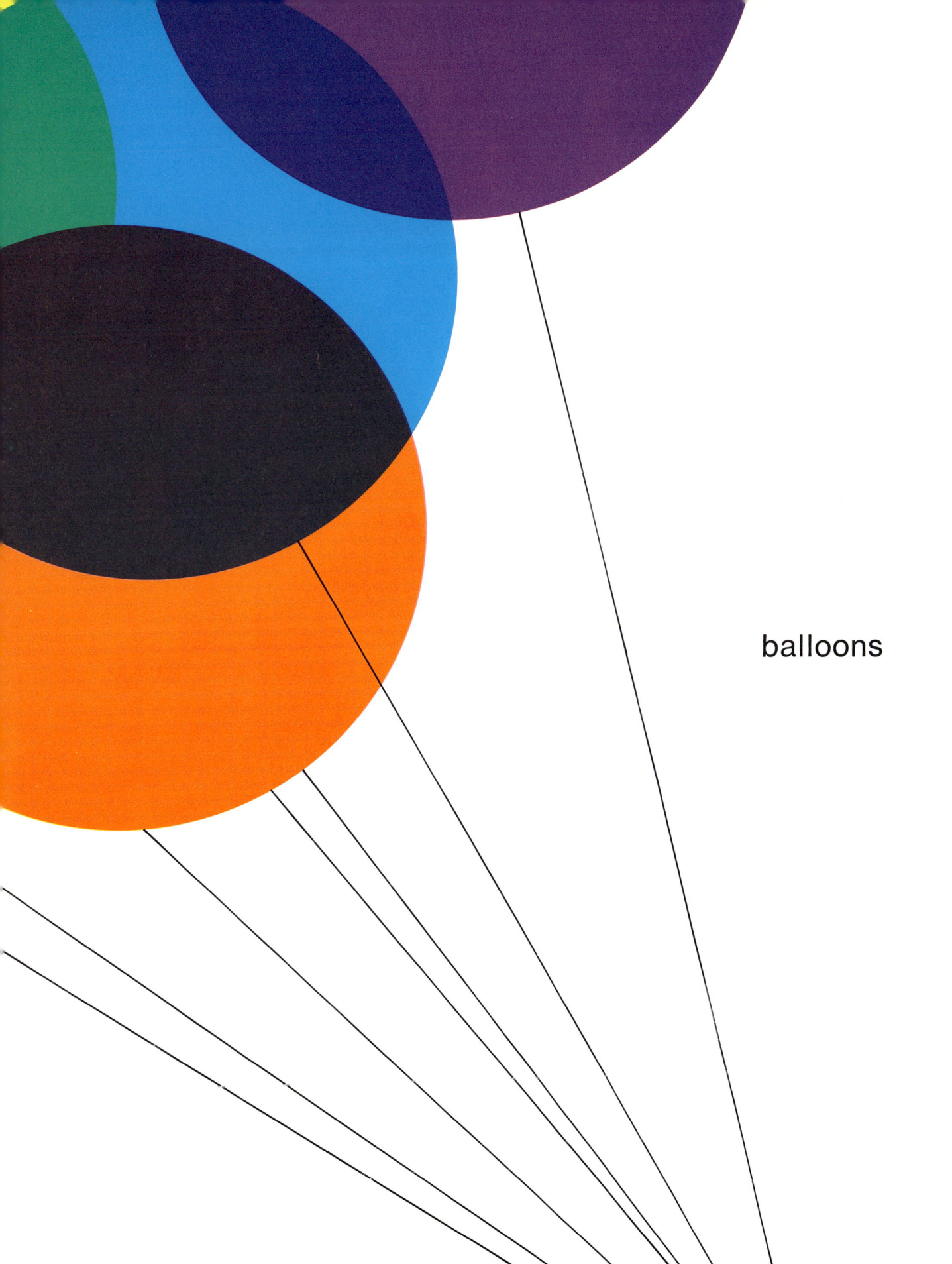

balloons

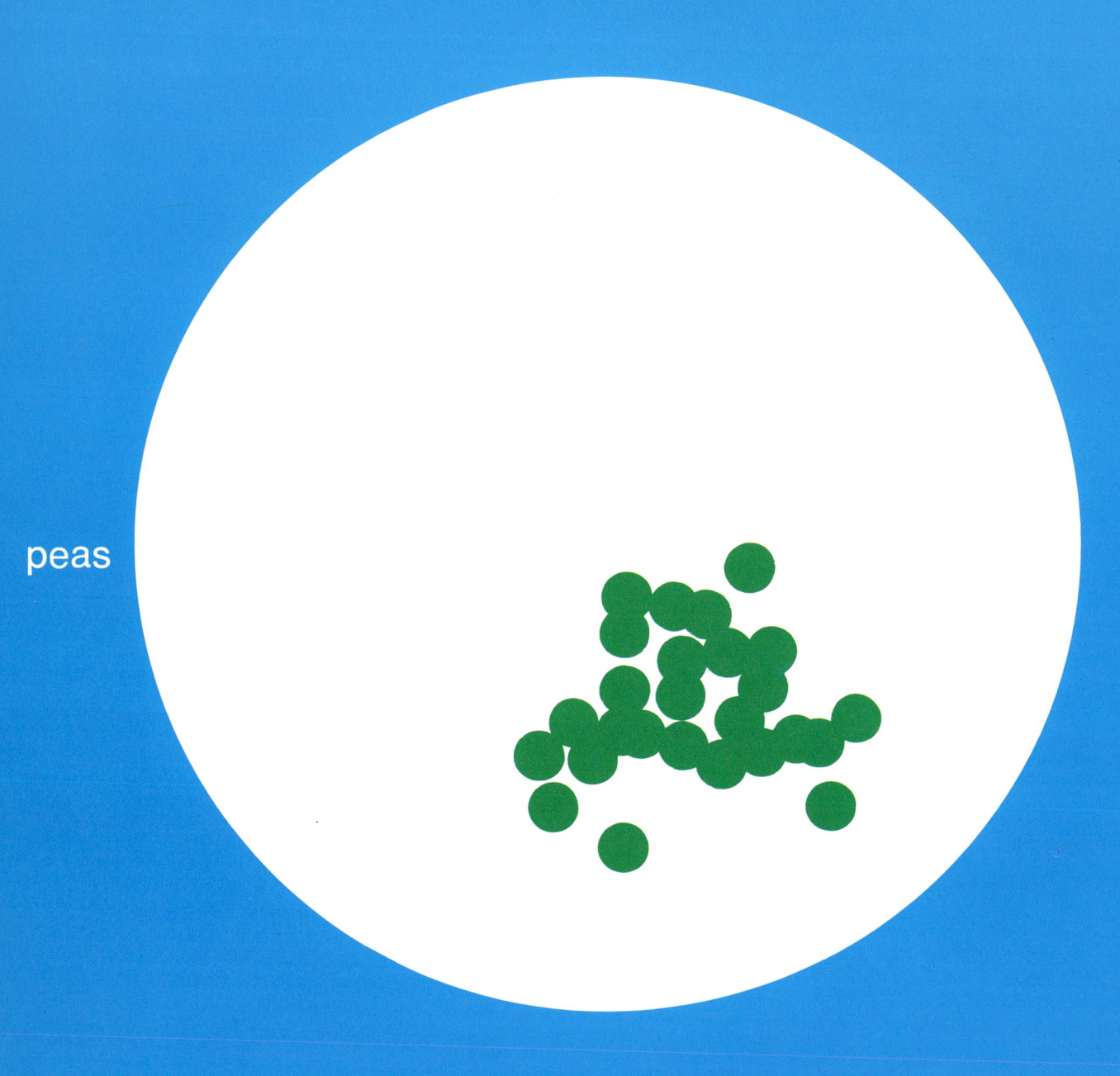

peas

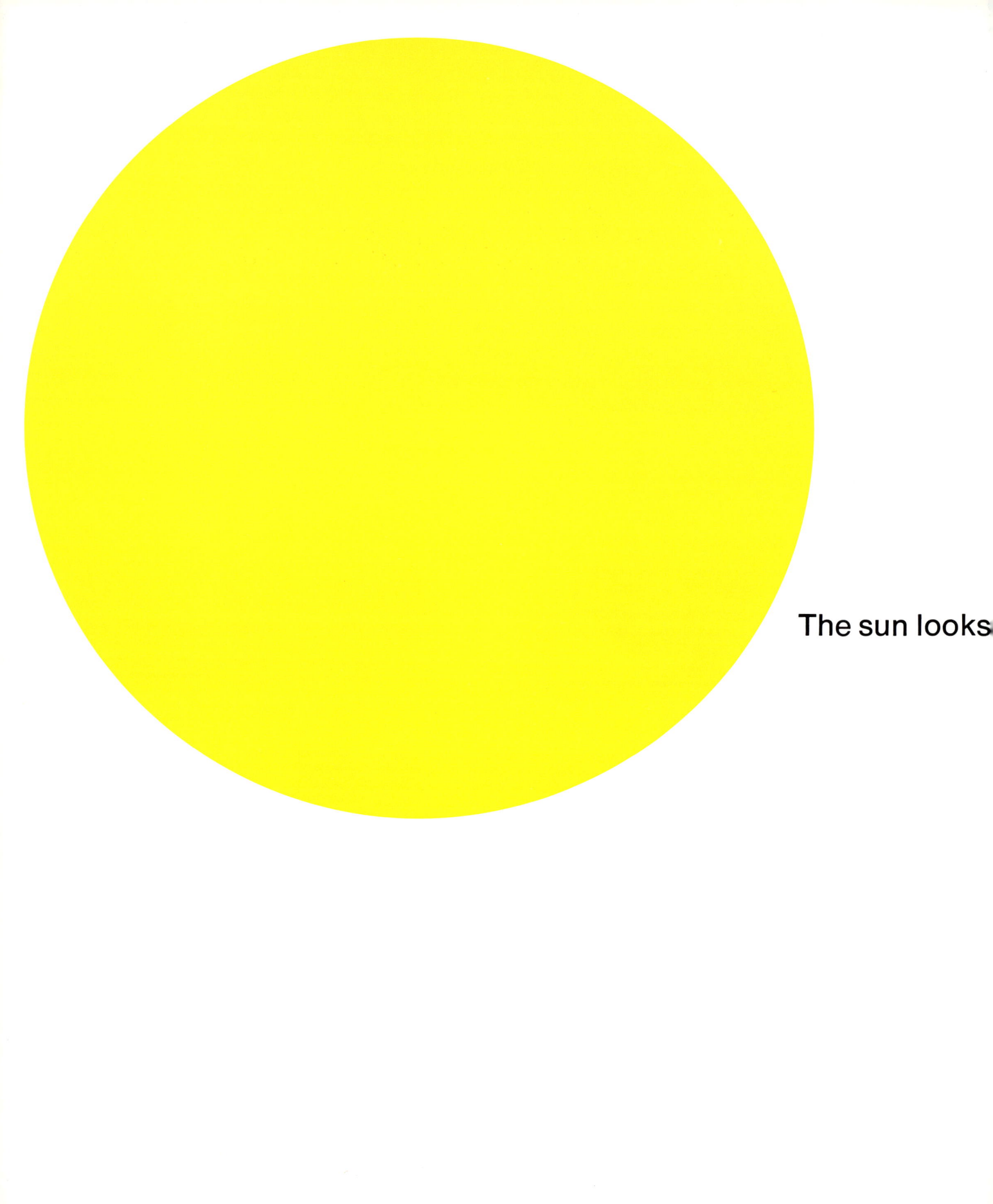

The sun looks

ike a circle.   We think of God who made it to warm us and to help . . .

flowers grow.

The moon looks like a circle

We think of God who protects us through the night and forever.

A ball looks like a circle. We think of God who brings fun and joy into our lives

nd wants us to be happy forever.

The world is like a line. It had a beginning

and it will end.

You and I began as a line begins. But when we come to the end o our line, we will find . . .

━━━━━━━━━━━━━━━━━━━ a circle.

## A NOTE TO PARENTS

As a parent you may find it difficult at times to answer your child's questions about birth, death, and eternal life. This book can help you talk with your child because it uses simple lines and circles to stimulate the imagination and open the mind.

Circles do not begin or end, but lines do have a beginning and an ending. Like a line, people have a beginning and an ending, but for us the end of life is different. "When we come to the end of our line we will find a circle."

What does this mean, that "we will find a circle" at the end of our line?

Human life does not disappear the way a line disappears at its end. At our "end" we meet God who lives forever. We are confident of life without end in the presence of God because we know that Jesus Christ overcame death. He arose from the grave and made eternal life possible. All who believe on the Lord Jesus Christ God will raise from death and give everlasting life.

This is not a book to be read only once. You may share it often and use it as an opportunity for discussion. Especially at the time of a death this book can be used to bring hope and assurance.

At the end of our lives we will find a circle. Thank God—and help your child thank God—for circles.